SACRAMENTO PUBLIC LIBRARY

D0722768

STARFISH

A Buddy Book by
Deborah Coldiron

ABDO
Publishing Company

UNDERWATER
WORLD

VISIT US AT
www.abdopublishing.com

Published by ABDO Publishing Company, 8000 West 78th Street, Edina, Minnesota 55439.

Copyright © 2008 by Abdo Consulting Group, Inc. International copyrights reserved in all countries. No part of this book may be reproduced in any form without written permission from the publisher. Buddy Books™ is a trademark and logo of ABDO Publishing Company.

Printed in the United States.

Coordinating Series Editor: Sarah Tieck
Contributing Editor: Michael P. Goecke
Graphic Design: Deborah Coldiron
Cover Photograph: Art Explosion
Interior Photographs/Illustrations: Clipart.com (page 11); Brandon Cole Marine Photography (page 9); Minden Pictures: Fred Bavendam (page 15), Frans Lanting (page 28), Chris Newbert (page 27), Flip Nicklin (page 29), D.P. Wilson/FLPA (page 17), Norbert Wu (pages 23, 25, 30); Photos.com (pages 5, 7, 13, 18, 19, 21)

Library of Congress Cataloging-in-Publication Data

Coldiron, Deborah.
    Starfish / Deborah Coldiron.
        p. cm. — (Underwater World)
    Includes index.
    ISBN 978-1-59928-813-0
    1. Starfishes—Juvenile literature. I. Title.

QL384.A8C65 2007
593.9'3—dc22
                                                                    2007016263

Table Of Contents

The World Of Starfish

Every living creature needs water. Some animals not only need water, they live in it, too.

Scientists have found more than 250,000 kinds of plants and animals living underwater. And, they believe there could be one million more! The starfish is one animal that makes its home in this underwater world.

Starfish come in many colors, patterns, and textures.

A Closer Look

Starfish are rather flat creatures with spiny skin. Some starfish have patterns that blend into their surroundings. Others have brightly colored skin.

FAST FACTS

Starfish belong to a group of animals known as echinoderms. Echinoderm means "spiny-skinned."

Every starfish has an opening called a madreporite (MA-druh-pawr-ite). Seawater enters this opening. Then, it moves throughout the starfish's body. The water gives the starfish's tube f the **suction** they need to grip and ove.

The madreporite is located near the center of a starfish's top side. Sometimes it appears as a large white spot.

Instead of a front and back side, a starfish has a top and bottom side. A starfish's mouth is located in the center of its bottom side.

The bottom side of a starfish is covered in hundreds of tiny tube feet. These feet work together to help the starfish walk. Starfish can walk in any direction. But, most move very slow.

Starfish Top Side

Arms

Madreporite

Tube Feet

Gills

Mouth

Tube Feet Row

Skin Spines

Eye Spot

Eye Spot

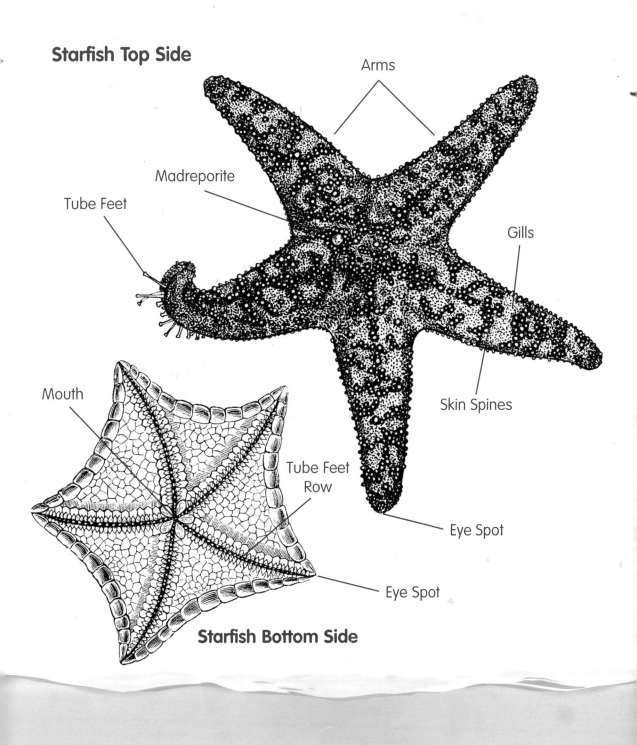

Starfish Bottom Side

Most starfish have five arms. At the end of each arm, there is a small eye spot. Starfish have very poor eyesight compared to humans. But, they use their eyes to sense changes in light. This helps them notice movements nearby.

FAST FACTS Starfish do not have brains or blood in their bodies.

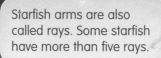

Starfish arms are also called rays. Some starfish have more than five rays.

A Growing Starfish

A starfish begins life as a tiny egg. Some starfish mothers release eggs in the water. Then, the eggs float freely.

Other starfish mothers **brood** their eggs. Brooding mothers may attach their eggs to their bodies. Some store them inside one of their two stomachs. Others find a place to attach their eggs to the seafloor.

FAST FACTS Starfish mothers can release millions of eggs at a time!

Deep-sea starfish are more likely to **brood** their eggs than starfish in warmer areas. That is because it is harder for starfish larvae to survive alone in cold, deep water.

To release their eggs into the ocean, starfish raise their bodies up high.

When starfish eggs hatch, tiny larval starfish **emerge**. These creatures look very different from their parents. At this life stage, they are **symmetrical**.

For about two months, the larval starfish float near the surface. They belong to a large group of other tiny creatures known as **plankton**.

As young starfish grow, they change shape. Eventually, they sink to the seafloor to live as adults.

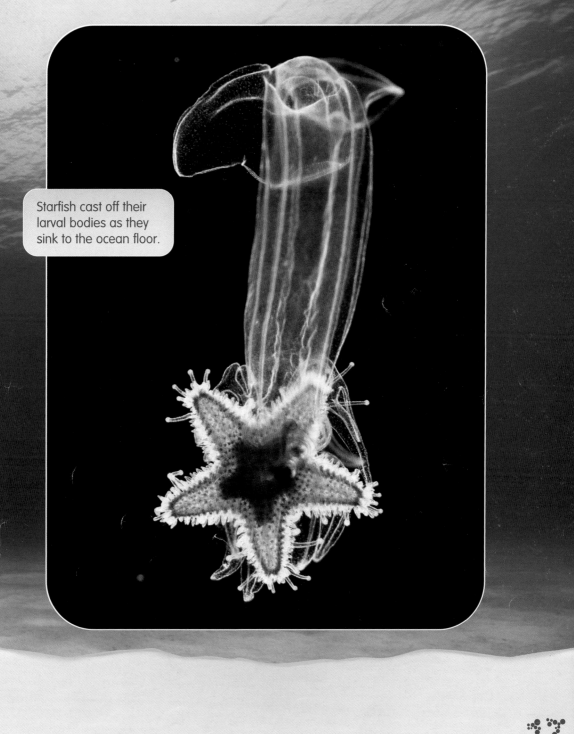

Starfish cast off their larval bodies as they sink to the ocean floor.

Family Connections

Echinoderms, such as starfish, have one major feature in common. They all have many tube feet!

Throughout the world, there are about 6,000 **species** of echinoderms. Other echinoderms include sand dollars, sea urchins, sea cucumbers, brittle stars, and feather stars.

Sand dollars are round, flat creatures covered in fuzzy, brown skin. But when dried, their skeletons are white and look like coins.

Brittle stars look much like starfish. But, the round shape of a brittle star's center is more apparent than a starfish's center.

Feather stars fix their bodies to the ocean floor. Then, they let their frilly arms sway in the water. This is how they catch tiny organisms to eat.

Sea urchins are round animals with long, sharp spines that move. Some species have spines that can be up to eight inches (20 cm) long.

There are about 500 species of sea cucumbers. Some can grow to be 24 to 36 inches (61 or 91 cm) long. If cornered by a predator, a sea cucumber can expel some of its internal organs. This can confuse its enemy and help it stay safe. Then, it grows new body parts.

Citizens Of The Sea

Starfish make their homes in a wide variety of **habitats**. They live in coral reefs, in kelp forests, and on the seafloor.

Starfish that live on the ocean floor have many different neighbors. Sea slugs, sea sponges, octopuses, and marine worms live near them. Lobsters, shrimp, sea anemones, coral, and crabs are also neighbors.

Starfish neighbors include sea sponges *(above)*, octopuses *(right)*, and lobsters *(below)*.

Picky Eaters

Starfish are meat eaters. Most starfish feed on mollusks, such as clams, oysters, and mussels. Some starfish eat sick or dead fish that have fallen to the seafloor. This is called scavenging.

Starfish eat in an unusual way. A starfish has two stomachs. It can push one stomach outside of its body to directly **digest** prey. Or, it can use its mouth to swallow the prey whole.

FAST FACTS

Starfish use the suction cups on their tube feet to pry open clam shells. Then, they slip one of their two stomachs into the shell to eat the clam.

Starfish scavenge on dead animals such as seals (*left*), and other starfish (*below*).

Some **species** of starfish are picky eaters. Certain deep-sea starfish only feed on **plankton**.

The crown-of-thorns starfish eats only coral. The bloody Henry starfish has **mucus**-coated skin that helps it catch tiny organisms to eat. It also feeds on sea sponges.

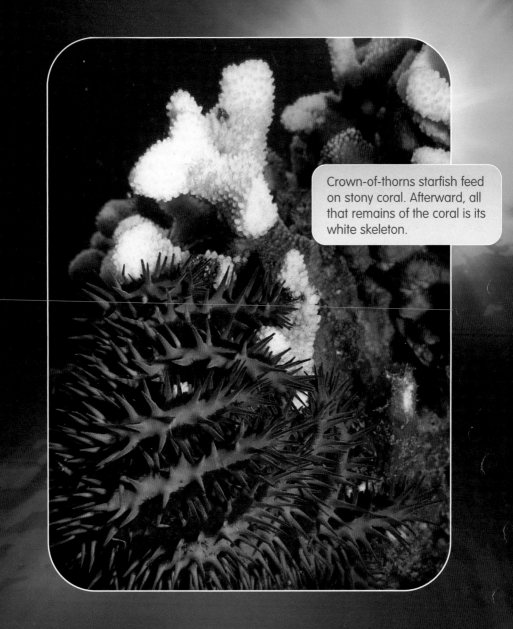

Crown-of-thorns starfish feed on stony coral. Afterward, all that remains of the coral is its white skeleton.

Danger Ahead!

Starfish are not popular food for ocean predators. Starfish have **toxins** in their bodies. These help protect them from predators. But, if a starfish is partially eaten, it can usually grow back the missing flesh. Despite these features, starfish still have a few enemies.

FAST FACTS If confronted with a predator, many starfish can drop an arm. This distracts the enemy while it escapes. Later, the starfish can regrow its lost limb.

Harlequin shrimp are enemies to some starfish. In fact, they eat starfish alive! Some scientists believe the shrimp actually feed starfish to keep them alive.

A harlequin shrimp may eat a starfish for more than a month before it dies.

Fascinating Facts

Sunflower starfish have thousands of tiny tube feet.

✶ The largest starfish in the world is the sunflower starfish. It has around 24 arms. It is also the fastest. This starfish can speed along at a rate of 10 feet (3 m) per minute!

✶ Starfish tube feet have strong **suction**. If a starfish is pulled from a rock, some of its tube feet may tear off and continue to cling to the rock!

Starfish can cling tightly to rocks and other surfaces.

✷ The number of arms a starfish has can vary even within a single **species**.

✷ Legend has it that unknowing fishers used to chop up bothersome starfish. Then, they threw them back into the sea. But, this didn't always kill the starfish. Starfish can reproduce through **regeneration**. So, it actually made more starfish!

Learn And Explore

Researchers at Cornell University in New York used starfish as inspiration for a new robot. In November 2006, they introduced the Starfish Robot.

The robot changes its walk if one of its limbs is damaged or lost. This is the first robot to learn to overcome an injury!

Some starfish can regrow as many as four of their five arms. These starfish are often called comets.

IMPORTANT WORDS

brood   to care for eggs.

digest   what a body does to change food into usable substances.

emerge   to come out into view.

habitat   where an animal lives in the wild.

invertebrate   an animal without backbone.

mucus   thick, slippery fluid from the body.

plankton   a group of very small plants and animals that float in the water. Many animals eat plankton.

regeneration   the act of replacing lost or injured tissues.

species   living things that are very much alike.

suction   to draw out using force.

symmetrical   having corresponding parts that are similar in shape, size, and position.

toxin   a harmful substance.

tropical   weather that is warm and wet.

WEB SITES

To learn more about starfish, visit ABDO Publishing Company on the World Wide Web. Web sites about starfish are featured on our Book Links page. These links are routinely monitored and updated to provide the most current information available.

www.abdopublishing.com

INDEX